# AUSTRALIAN BUSES AND COACHES

TONY FINNERAN

First published 2022

Amberley Publishing
The Hill, Stroud
Gloucestershire, GL5 4EP

www.amberley-books.com



ISBN 978 1 3981 0512 6 (print)
ISBN 978 1 3981 0513 3 (ebook)



British Library Cataloguing in Publication Data.
A catalogue record for this book is available from the British Library.

Typesetting by SJmagic DESIGN SERVICES, India.
Printed in Great Britain.

# Introduction

Australia's bus and coaches over the decades are presented in colour photos from my collection. Australia's Commonwealth is made up of five states and two territories. There is a representation of a bus or coach from each state and territory. The vehicles are listed in chronological order of the build date from the bodybuilder. Australia has many depot-built bodies that utilised mainly ex-Government chassis and rebodied these. Many of these in-house bodybuilders are displayed.

American and British chassis were generally used pre- and post-Second World War. From the 1960s a preference emerged for British chassis. The 1970s saw a European invasion influenced by the Volvo and Mercedes chassis. They made the British vehicles seem antiquated. Other than the Leyland Tiger, the European chassis dominated the market, complimented by Japanese chassis and Australian-built chassis utilising American drive train.

The Australian bodybuilders used various innovative designs to cope with our heat, dust, snow fields and long distances operated at high speeds. Most of these are represented in this book. Bodybuilders manufactured in every state, some being built in Brisbane and then delivered to Perth, a distance of around 4,500 km (2,800 miles). Their first service were due on arrival.

My career was a New South Wales-based bus chassis salesman for Saab Scania Australia, Ansair, MAN Automotive and back to Scania Australia. I enjoyed this job for over thirty years and made many long lasting relationships where customers became friends instead of just a commercial relationship. I'll try and explain this through the various captions.

There are over 150 bus operators, twenty chassis types, over 100 chassis models and over seventy-five bodybuilders listed in this publication.

For those of you who don't know me, I have been in the operations side with companies such as AAT (Grenda-Pykes Tours-Blue Line era), Ansett Pioneer, Deanes Coaches and Clipper Tours. Then selling chassis and bodies, all this while also serving for over thirty-seven years in the Australian Army Reserve.

I have written the Gone but not Forgotten series about elements of the Australian bus and coach industry (gbnf.com.au).

Nearly eight years ago on Easter Sunday in March 2013 I suffered a severe stroke and was paralysed for the first month. The South West Sydney Local Health District of NSW (Sydney Metro area) saved my life and then gave me back my mobility. I'm left with a few deficiencies like a 'dodgy' right hand and a loss of all my peripheral vision. I'm a very lucky boy!

Many of these images were taken with 'Box Brownie', 126-, 110- and 135-mm film. In my early days I couldn't afford a good-quality camera. Although some images are fuzzy, I think you will find the selection quite comprehensive and worthwhile to have in your collection.

Melbourne Metropolitan Tramways Board's (MMTB) fleet number 370 (ET 370), a Leyland OPS1 with MMTB Prestons Workshops (VIC) bodywork, built in 1948. It is a restoration bus in the old livery used in the 1954 Olympic Games. Sadly, it had been a rainy morning earlier in Melbourne during the historic vehicle parade.

Red Transit Co., Hurstville, Sydney Metro. M/O 507, an Albion Valkyrie CX 13L with Star Brothers (NSW) bodywork, built in 1948. This ornate bus plied the streets of the south-west Sydney suburbs between Hurstville and Hurstville Grove. It is now a prominent display at the Sydney Bus Museum.

Toronto Bus Service, Toronto, NSW. M/O 4160, an AEC Regent III with Comeng (NSW) bodywork, built in 1948. This ex-NSW Government double-decker was formerly MO 2092. This bus originally had an open rear platform. However, Toronto enclosed it for the safety of schoolchildren.

Lever Coach Lines, Queanbeyan. MO 3101, a White 798 fully imported American city bus, built in 1948. Originally trialed by the New South Wales Government, it was eventually sold to Quodling Bros and inherited by Levers, becoming the pride of the fleet. It was repowered by a 505 AEC.

West End Bus Service, Townsville. Deregistered Q/T plate 1408, a Bedford OB with locally built Skuderi (QLD) bodywork, was built around 1948. This rounded look was considered a very smart appearance in its heyday. Townsville is located in Far North Queensland.

Scholes Motor Service, Merewether, NSW. M/O 147, a White with MBA (NSW) bodywork, built in 1949. This White was used for an industrial service to and from Stewarts and Lloyds, a steel fabrication factory in Newcastle from 1920 to 1970.

McVicar's Bus Service, Lidcombe, Sydney Metro. M/O 516, an Albion Valiant CX39LW with Comeng (Commonwealth Engineering NSW) bodywork, built in 1950. McVicar's operated a large fleet in Sydney's western and south-western suburbs through suburbs like Revesby, Padstow and East Hills. They were one of Sydney's largest private operators in their time during the mid-1970s.

Glen Charter Coaches, Glen Innes. This is a deregistered White WC16 with Syd Wood (NSW) bodywork, built in 1951. Pat O'Dea, Bus salesman with Bedford dealer Suttons, complained about Sutton's (a Bedford dealer) trade-ins being tampered with – for example good tyres swapped with worn tyres after the deal was done. This was a Sutton's trade-in, with a January delivery.

Mount Dandenong Passenger Service, Melbourne. Fleet number 10 (GBW 823), a Leyland OPS4/1 with Watt Bros (QLD) bodywork, built in 1952. This was a classic body style for ex-Palmer's Overland, an interstate long-distance operation. The bus is seen on display in Melbourne preserved for future generations.

West End Bus Service, Townsville, QLD. PFY 448, a Bedford OB with CAC (Commonwealth Aircraft Corporation – VIC) bodywork, was built around 1950. General Motors Holden distributed these Bedford buses and had in-house financing for both new and used buyers. These were a very popular bus on Australian roads.

Department of Government Transport, Sydney, NSW. M/O 2807, an AEC Regal IV 9821E with Comeng (NSW) bodywork, built in 1954. This was used during Queen Elizabeth II's tour to Australia after her coronation. The bus is now preserved with the Sydney Bus Museum and was recently seen at the Bankstown Air Show conducting vintage bus rides.

The Entrance Red Bus Services, The Entrance, NSW. MO 076, Fleet 23 Reo with Properts (NSW) bodywork, built in 1952. The recessed window line and pronounced destination box are two key identifiers for a Properts body around this time. The bus was used for school services when the photo was taken.

Public Transport Commission (PTC), Ryde Depot, Sydney Metro, NSW. M/O 2874, an AEC Regent III 9612E with Comeng (NSW) bodywork, built in 1954. This bus was a staff change over bus and would run up from Ryde Depot to Victoria Road and change drivers for rest breaks. It is seen waiting for its next mission.

The Entrance Red Bus Services, The Entrance, NSW. MO 224, Fleet 22 Reo with Syd Wood (NSW) bodywork, built in 1955. These were taken at The Entrance depot in the early 1970s when these buses were still performing daily school runs during the school terms.

The Entrance Red Bus Service, The Entrance, NSW. This deregistered Mack with Syd Wood (NSW) bodywork was built in 1955. This bus had been sold by Entrance Red to a bus preservation owner who restored it and brought it back to Red Bus for temporary storage. The Mack chassis would have been a war surplus disposal truck chassis. They had a very narrow bridge at The Entrance and these headlights kept on being damaged by the drivers.

Red Coaches, The Entrance, NSW. MO 359, Fleet 9 Reo with Properts (NSW) bodywork, was built around 1955. The Holden grill was for decoration and style, although, in my opinion, a Ford grill would have been better. The roof racks were for luggage from either Gosford or Wyong railway stations.

Alice Springs Bus Service, NT. M/O 176 (N/T), a Foden PVSC6 with Motor Body Assemblers (MBA, NSW) bodywork, built in 1956. This bus previously operated overland services from Adelaide to Darwin. It is seen in the depot having been relegated to school bus duties some thirty years after its prime.

Watt Brothers Bus Service, Wollongong. M/O 6165, an AEC Reliance 470 with Hughes, Whetton and Riley (NSW) bodywork, built in 1956. This bodybuilder manufactured in Wollongong and had attractive designs as demonstrated by this AEC.

The Entrance Red Bus Services, The Entrance. MO 3565, Fleet 7 Reo with Syd Wood (NSW) bodywork, built in 1956. This bus always impressed me. It looked rugged and tough and originally was used for tours in the Snowy Mountains scheme. No. 7 gave honest service to Red Bus for many years.

Melbourne Metropolitan Tramways Board (MMTB). Fleet number 623 (GRA 623), an AEC Regal IV with Lawton (VIC) bodywork, built in 1956. Photographed on a rain-soaked day after completing Route 246 to Clifton Hill. They were purchased for the 1956 Olympic Games to service the Olympic Village in West Heidelberg.

Private buyer, Townsville, QLD. This deregistered Commer TS 3 with Lawton (SA) bodywork was built around 1956. This bus was originally used as an airporter for Australian National Airlines and the hump back was used to store luggage in a boot while giving passengers their first experience of airline service.

Linsley's Motors, Wallsend, NSW. M/O 5314, an AEC Regal IV 9823E with Lawton (SA) bodywork, built in 1955. This bus was used on industrial services, route and school services. Linsley's relied heavily on ex-Government buses in the fleet. This was ex-MTT (Adelaide) 732.

Bowman's Bus Service operated in the St Mary's area of Sydney. M/O 467, a Leyland Comet with Hughes, Whetton & Riley (HWR – NSW) bodywork built in 1957. This photo was taken at Llandilo and was looking to be sold as a shed or motor home conversion.

John J. Hill, Wollongong, NSW. M/O 6272, an AEC Regal IV with CBW (Tasmanian) bodywork, was built around 1957. John J's, like most of the Wollongong operators, purchased second-hand Government buses to supplement their fleets. These also had subtle variations in the livery pattern from the rest of the fleet.

Rover Motors, Cessnock, NSW. MO 5708 (fleet number 10), an AEC Regent with Comeng (NSW) bodywork, was built around 1960. This was a rebody of a former AEC decker ex-Government. I met Rab Lewis at a BCA First Generation Conference in Leura (Blue Mountains, NSW) in around 1989. He gave me lots of time explaining life in the early days in Cessnock.

Darwin Bus and Motor Service, M/O 411 (NT), a Bedford SBG with CAC (GMH) from Victoria round screen bodywork, was built around 1957. These are recognised as 'The' Australian bus at the time. During the post-war years public transport was a necessity for families and workers commuting in their daily lives.

MTT, Adelaide, South Australia. 450 823, a Leyland Worldmaster CRT2/1 with Lawton (SA) bodywork, was built around 1957. These three-door buses were purpose-built city buses and the Adelaide design was quite distinctive. This bus had been sold from the MTT and was located at Dion's Bus Service depot in Wollongong, NSW.

Public Transport Commission, Sydney. M/O 3013, a Leyland Royal Tiger Worldmaster ERT1/1 with CCMC (NSW) bodywork, built in 1957. These buses featured similar styling to the American Mack design and common in Sweden with the Scania Vabis C70 Capitol bus. The NSW Government had numerous public transport authority name changes and liveries over the years.

Mercury Roadlines, Kempsey, NSW. MO 4183, a Leyland Comet with Mercury (NSW) bodywork, was built around 1958. A personal favourite photo with this old 'banger' backed up to the parcel shed at Kempsey station loading freight to the coast before collecting the passengers for the South West Rocks service.

Robert's Brisbane Water Coaches, Gosford, NSW. MO 4828 (fleet number 15), a Bedford SB3 with CCMC (NSW) bodywork, built in 1959. Previously a tour coach, this CCMC body shows the earlier Bedford grill cowl that was used for all Bedfords at that time. Robert's had an attractive livery at this time.

Moore's Tours, Arncliffe, Sydney Metro, NSW. M/O 4038, an AEC Regal Mk 4 9823E with Clyde (NSW) bodywork, was built around 1958. This was ex-DGT 3417 and these buses always had their nearside rear view mirror located at the side window behind the driver after the front door. These bodies also introduced large air vents to the front of the bus for our hot days.

Fogg's Motor Service, Maitland, NSW. M/O 4294, an AEC Reliance 470 2HMU2RA with Syd Wood (NSW) bodywork, built in 1960. This bus operated the Lemon Tree Passage service after being retired from coach duties. Love the rounded windows that can be achieved with a timber frame.

Riverstone Bus Service, Sydney. M/O 4319, a White FC with Parramatta Ryde (NSW) bodywork, built in 1960. This bus had been repowered with a Bedford 330 diesel engine. It operated in the far western suburbs of Sydney. Parramatta Ryde Bus Service built their own bodies.

South & Western Coach Lines (Revesby), NSW. M/O 4534, Leyland Royal Tiger Worldmaster with Bolton (WA) bodywork, built in 1960. This bus was ex-MTT Perth 259 and many made the 4,000 km journey to the east coast to continue their working lives. South and Western had two depots within the Sydney Metro area.

Stone Bros Bus Service, Auburn, Sydney Metro. M/O 4346, an AEC Mammoth Major with Stone Bros (NSW) bodywork, built in 1960. Stone Bros had the nickname of 'Stone Age Transport' within parts of the industry. They built their own bodies and often incorporated the AEC truck grill painted in a contrast colour. I like them.

Robert's Brisbane Water Coaches, Gosford, NSW. M/O 7141 (fleet number 20), a Reo FE with Syd Wood (NSW) bodywork, built in 1960. These Forward Entry (FE) Reos were reasonably rare and these ex-Hunters Hill (in Sydney) buses were powered by Perkins engines.

Robert's Brisbane Water Coaches, Gosford, NSW. MO 7699 (fleet number 27) a White with Parramatta Ryde (NSW) bodywork, was built around 1961. The Robert's livery really suited these Parramatta Ryde bodies. White's were purchased second hand by Robert's to cope with high patronage from local schools.

Barklimore Bros Bus Service, Merrylands, Sydney. M/O 4474 is White FC with Syd Wood bodywork of 1961. This would have been one of the last bodies built by the Bankstown (NSW) timber-framed builder Syd Wood. Steel frames were the fashion and more accepted by the Australian operators.

Green's Northern Coaches, Thirroul, NSW. M/O 6215, a Leyland Royal Tiger Cub RTC1/1 with Comair (VIC) bodywork, built in 1961. This photo was taken in the depot with the Bulli escarpment looking towards Stanwell Tops in the background. Another bus acquired from Hills Bus Service, Fairy Meadow.

Department of Government Transport (DGT), NSW. M/O 3499, an AEC Regal Mk 4 9823E with Clyde (NSW) bodywork, built in 1961. Although these buses were built to a fairly standard pattern, a few ideas were experimented with such as the roof vents on 3499 to take the heat out of the bus on hot days.

Chester Hill Bankstown Bus Service, Sydney, NSW. M/O 130, Bedford SB 5 with CCMC (Cycle Component Manufacturing Company, NSW) Mk 1 bodywork, built in 1962. This was my local bus service when I was growing up and I thought their livery was very handsome.

Camden Bus Service, Melbourne, VIC. Fleet number 12 (HRW 396), Bedford SB3 with Comair (VIC) bodywork, built in 1962. New to Eastern Suburbs Omnibus Service, this bus was delivered with a centre door but no front door. The 'shark front' was a distinctive body style by Comair. This photo was taken on a mission to Melbourne with Ray Boddenberg in 1979.

Melbourne Brighton Bus Lines, Melbourne Metro, VIC. Fleet number 62 (HNW 262), a Leyland Royal Tiger Cub with Comair (VIC) bodywork, built in 1962. This photo was again taken in the evening on a rainy Melbourne day. It has recently returned to the depot after completing Route 601 to St Kilda railway station. Note the coloured roof lights, unique to MBBL, that are used to denote which route by colours at night.

Alice Springs Bus Service, NT. Fleet number 40 (M/O 763 (NT)), a Leyland Tiger Cub with Freighter (Adelaide, SA) bodywork, was built around 1962. This looks like a whole assortment of bodies mixed into the one body – elements of MBA with the roof dome, Freighter front and Ansair-style windscreens.

South Townsville Bus Service, QLD. OPE 119, a Bedford SB 3 with Athol Hedges (Brisbane, QLD) bodywork, was built around 1962. The Bedford cowl was still being utilised by some of the bodybuilders, although most were beginning to move to create their own grill and style as we will see later on.

Camden Coaches, NSW. MO 7235 Bedford SB 5 (Quasi control) with Coachmaster (Peakhurst, NSW) bodywork, built *c.* 1962. Australians wanted larger buses and we modified SB chassis to be VAM like with forward entry (FE) to obtain a larger seating capacity. Braking capacity remained unchanged from standard.

Lever Coach Lines, Queanbeyan, NSW. This deregistered Reo with CCMC (NSW) Mk 1 bodywork was built around 1962. This classic bus remained in the fleet for many years. Its high back seats were used for the Canberra–Queanbeyan Charter division. It's simply a good-looking bus with a great livery.

Peakhurst and Lugarno Bus Companies (H.T. Saints & Sons Pty Ltd), Sydney. M/O 4630 Atkinson Alpha BPL746H with Coachmaster (NSW) bodywork, built in 1963. This bus is on a charter and laid up under the Sydney Harbour Bridge pylons. At the time Saints were a highly respected Sydney operator.

Western Road Bus Service Pty Ltd operated in the Parramatta and Blacktown areas of Sydney. M/O 4605, a Bedford SB5 with CCMC (NSW) Mk 2 bodywork, built in 1964. Western Road was another one of the large family-owned businesses in Sydney's western suburbs.

Moonee Valley Bus Lines, Melbourne Metro. Fleet number 22 (JCH 807), a Bedford SB5 with Freighter (SA) bodywork, built in 1964. On a rainy day this bus is waiting at the terminus in Moonee Ponds waiting to perform Route 506 with a good passenger load on board.

Punchbowl Bus Company, Riverwood, NSW. M/O 886, a Leyland Royal Tiger Cub RTC 1/2 with Coachmaster (NSW) bodywork, built in 1964. Punchbowl was owned at this time by Joe Griffin, who was a wonderful gentleman. They operated in the south-western Sydney suburbs.

Hermit Park Bus Service, Townsville, QLD. 233 NKQ, a Leyland Leopard with Ansair (VIC) bodywork, built in 1964. Originally this bus was doing school services and snow fields tours from Cooma (NSW) with Ansett Pioneer. It went through an operator in Sydney before its move to Far North Queensland.

State Transit Authority, NSW. M/O 3520, a Leyland Leopard PSU3/2RT with Chullora Workshops (NSW) bodywork, built in 1964. An experimental bus for use in Sydney and among its features when new were fibreglass seats, forced air ventilation and a new body design. Chullora Workshops were the repair shop for all Government buses. This bus was known as 'Mr Whippy'.

Ansett Pioneer, NT. Fleet number 660 (ORZ 977), a GMC PD-4106 with GMC (USA) bodywork, built in 1964. These right-hand-drive converted American coaches were arguably the best vehicles on the road in Australia. Their road handling and suspension were second to none. This coach is fitted with 'Bat Wings' on the air intake for the engine to overcome dust in the engine.

Ansett Pioneer, NSW. A GMC PD-4106, 664 is one of the batch of second-hand American units purchased from Hawaii (USA). In my opinion they were the best coaches on the road for the era with air suspension, air conditioning and a GM 8V71 engine with a four-speed gearbox. This one is in 1770 Bicentennial livery (USA).

Parramatta Ryde Bus Services, Sydney Metro. M/O 5000, an AEC Reliance 590 with Parramatta Ryde (NSW) bodywork, built in 1966. Parramatta Ryde built their own bodies and these AECs had a distinctive design created by Ivan Ferris, a partner in the business. I found them unusual and attractive.

Moore's Tours, Gymea, Sydney Metro. M/O 4985 Leyland Tiger Cub PSU3/1R with Comeng (NSW) bodywork, built in 1966. This bus gave terrific service to the Moore family so much so that the family has decided to restore and preserve the family favourite at the time of this publication.

Fangia Bus Lines, Tonga. This deregistered Bedford SB5 with TRC (NSW) bodywork built in 1966. TRC was a short-lived bus builder who used components from Redman Mitchell Co. (QLD) bodies. This was formerly MO 44 with Moore's Tours and although the Tongans generally bought Albion Viking, this was destined for export.

Matilda Tours, Darwin, NT. MO 477, an Albion Viking VK 41 with Freighter (SA) bodywork, was built around 1966. This old coach had been sold on and relegated to school duties in the Northern Territory. Freighter bodies were very tough and front engine Vikings with a Freighter body were highly sought after by outback operators.

Redcliffe Peninsula, Redcliffe, QLD. Fleet number 59 (PMD 736), a Hino RC 320P with Freighter (SA) step deck bodywork, was built around 1966. A great colour scheme for this older coach was used for a longer Brisbane route service. The Hino chassis had inboard air bag suspension without sway bars and rolled considerably through winding roads.

Sainty's Coaches, Launceston, TAS. AA 8812, a Leyland Tiger OPS 1 with Freighter (SA) bodywork, built in 1967. This was a rebodied front engine Leyland and the rebody was new to Sellick from Adelaide. It was an unusual rebody that worked quite well for many years.

Fearnes Coaches, Wagga Wagga, NSW. MO 4639, a Leyland Leopard PSU3/1RT with Denning (QLD) 'Square' bodywork, built in 1967. Owned by the Fearne family, they were well respected in the community and had a passenger terminal in the new depot. I never liked the Denning Square body style.

Public Transport Commission (Brookvale), NSW. M/O 3556, a Leyland Leopard PSU3/2R with PMC Sydney Mk 1 bodywork, built in 1967. Originally assigned to the PTC Newcastle operation, this bus had been transferred to the Brookvale depot. Newcastle buses had double dipped waistbands plus a shorter bumper than the same Sydney bus.

Rover Motors, Cessnock. NSW. Fleet number 2 (MO 7751), a Leyland Panther PSUR1/2R with Comeng Vehicle Industries (CVI – NSW) 'Capitol' bodywork, built in 1967. This bus was a former coach and at the time of the photo it had returned to the depot at Cessnock after completing a route from Newcastle a distance of some 50 km (31 miles).

Road Runner, Darwin, NT. M/O 419 (NT), an Albion Viking VK 41L with Watt Bros (NSW) bodywork, was built around 1967. These rear-stepped deck bodies were unusual and generally used for luggage space at the rear under the floor line. The addition of a centre door is also an unusual specification.

Alice Springs Bus Service, NT. MO 467. a Bedford J Series truck conversion with Motor Body Builders (WA) bodywork, was built around 1967. This bodybuilder had a short-term presence in our market and didn't have the most attractive body styles, although beauty is in the eye of the beholder.

Campbell's Coaches, Mt Isa, QLD. 028 NAF, an AEC Reliance with R. E. Mee bodywork, was built around 1967. R. E. Mee built for their own bus and coach business in Melbourne while also building bodies to order for other bus operations or suppliers. There are never too many angles on a Mee body – they're quite distinctive.

MTT Tasmania (Hobart) GT 8379, a Bedford SB3 with City Body Works (CBW Tasmania) bodywork, built in 1968. Tasmania had a large fleet of the lighter Bedford chassis after previously having AEC and Trolley buses. After this period they decided to purchase heavier chassis such as Hino, Volvo and Scania. They also transitioned from a green/cream livery to variations of this colour scheme.

Lehman, Peter, Candelo, NSW. MO 8028, a Leyland Leopard PSU3/2R with PMC Sydney bodywork, built in 1968. It has a vivid livery with numerous stripes in various colours with a yellow base. The PMC body had glass vents at the front to let air in. This bus ran from Bega to Candelo, a 25 km trip.

Red Transit Company, Hurstville Grove, in Sydney Metro. M/O 597, an AEC Regent III 9621A with Coachmaster (NSW) bodywork, built in 1968. This chassis was rebodied, having previously had a timber-framed Comemg body. It was a short route operating from Hurstville railway station to the village of Hurstville Grove, which is bound by the Georges River.

Brisbane City Council (BCC), QLD. Fleet number 472 (PWA 472). Leyland Panther PSUR1-1 with Athol Hedges (QLD) bodywork, built in 1968. Brisbane City Council operates the major routes in Brisbane and these Panthers were also built by Denning with the same pattern. They gave very good service to the council and this bus is seen in the revised yellow livery.

Ansett Pioneer's (Adelaide depot) fleet number 727 (KKO 054), a GMC PD-4107 'Jumbo' with GMC (USA) bodywork, built in 1968. This express unit is seen with the smaller original windows from GMC and locally adapted with the fitment of a 'Bull Bar', used to protect the front of the bus from stray livestock or more commonly kangaroos. A fantastic unit.

Ayers' Coach Services, Hobart, TAS. NB 6656, an AEC Reliance with Ansair (VIC) bodywork, was built around 1968. Tasmania during these years up until the millennium relied on the second-hand market to meet their needs. Government funds were very limited and the private operators had to choose wisely for vehicles to suit the task (e.g. charter or school bus).

Nicholson Bros Pennant Hills, Sydney Metro. M/O 845, a Ford R226 with Comeng Vehicle Industries (CVI – Sydney) 'Goldstar' bodywork, was built around 1968. This bus is on a charter (private hire) and had dropped off school children to the Sydney Opera House and relocated to the bus parking area at the time in Hickson Road under the Sydney Harbour Bridge. What a city Sydney is – come and visit us!

Foley's Bus Service, Kogarah, Sydney Metro. M/O 4705, an AEC Swift AH 505 MP3R with Athol Hedges (QLD) bodywork, built in 1969. This bus was formerly in Canberra with the ACTION fleet as ZIB 152. Z prefixes on registrations indicated a Commonwealth Government-owned vehicle. Later in 1988 the ACT became self-governing and remains the home of the Australian Parliament.

Deane's Coaches, North Ryde, Sydney Metro. M/O 5538, an Albion Viking VK41 with PMC Sydney bodywork, built in 1969. R. M. Campbell were bus dealers in Bankstown, NSW, and sold Austin, Albion and Leyland chassis. Campbell sold PMC bodies and had their own name plate under the chassis name, a 'fancy' grill and generally were loyal to PMC Sydney. This was an R. M. Campbell-sold bus.

Calabro Bros, Bonnyrigg, Sydney Metro. M/O 5390 White Quasi FC with CCMC (Guildford, Sydney) Mk 4 bodywork, built in 1969. This was a rebodied White converted to a front entry and must have been the last White to be rebodied in Australia. Calabro's repowered it with a Leyland 400 engine too.

Dion's Bus Service, Wollongong, NSW. M/O 6109, a Leyland Comet with Dion (Wollongong, NSW) bodywork, built in 1969. Dion's had built their own bodies for many years and were similar to the Syd Wood designs of the early 1960s. This body was built to their own design on a refurbished Leyland Comet chassis that had always given Dion's very honest service.

East Preston Bus Service, Epping, Melbourne Metro. Fleet number 6 (KEN 114) Bedford SB3 with Comair (VIC) bodywork, built in 1969. This bus had the new square back design of the Comair but didn't receive the latter grill style you will see later in this book. Petrol engines were still sought by this operator at this time and they were the last Melbourne operation to select diesel engines.

Kogarah Bus Service, Kogarah, Sydney Metro. M/O 5537, an AEC Reliance 505 6MU4RE with Coachmaster (NSW) bodywork, built in 1969. This bus is dropping off schoolchildren at Circular Quay and one can just see glimpses of the Sydney Opera House sails in the background. Note the head rests fitted to the seats. This bus is from the St George district and the crest is of St George slaying a dragon.

Royal Australian Navy, Garden Island, Sydney, NSW. ZIB 222, an Albion Viking VK 43 with Cheetham & Borwick (VIC) bodywork, built in 1969. Cheetham & Borwick generally built for Victorian operators, although they must have tendered to supply this bus to the Navy. The Navy grey doesn't do the body justice in the evening light.

Sydney by Night, North Ryde, Sydney Metro. MFN 159, a Leyland Atlantean PDR1/2A with PMC Sydney bodywork, built in 1970. Deane's Clipper Tours purchased Sydney by Night from Ansett Pioneer and at the time of the photo it was being sanded back waiting for its next paint design. Interesting to see it in this state. This Atlantean was purchased from the NSW Government Urban Transit Authority (UTA).

Bass Hill Bus Service, Bass Hill Sydney Metro. M/O 892 Bedford VAM 70 with CVI (Granville, Sydney) bodywork, built in 1970. When I was at school we often got these buses nicknamed a tunnel bus to our sport days. They were very stylish at the time and made a great impression. Sadly CVI were soon to sell out their designs to Smithfield Bus and Coach works and the design was short-lived.

Bankstown Lakemba Bus Service, Greenacre, Sydney Metro. M/O 505, a Bedford VAM 70 with Motor Body Specialists (MBS – QLD) bodywork, built in 1970. Bankstown Lakemba was operated by one of my favourite owners Bob Stephens, who started his bus and coach businesses from this humble start. Bob went on to own Bankstown Coaches and Challenge Coaches.

Cairns Trans, Cairns, QLD. 256 ANM, an AEC Swift with Denning (SA) bodywork, was built around 1971. These ex-South Australian Government (STA) buses went to all corners of Australia when disposed of. You may have noticed that each Government operation developed their own unique style of bodies that suited their particular passenger market.

Public Transport Commission (PTC) Ryde Depot, Sydney Metro. M/O 1143, a Leyland Atlantean PDRA1/1 with PMC Sydney bodywork, was built around 1971. This buses were meant for one-man operation but the body design was always going to be a two-man operation. This photo was taken outside my family home when my adopted brother 'Freddy Freeloader' was off route.

Parramatta Ryde Bus Service, West Ryde, Sydney Metro. M/O 5808, an Leyland Leopard PSU3A/2R with Parramatta Ryde (NSW) bodywork, built in 1972. This was my personal favourite body style of Parra Ryde using the Leyland Ergomatic truck grill. It had such a nice style and even with the dull background in this image, the bus looks great!

Chester Hill Bankstown Bus Service, Chester Hill, Sydney Metro. M/O 5827, a Bedford VAL 70 with Custom Coaches (NSW) bodywork, built in 1972. This was originally an English chassis imported into Australia by Hills Bus Sales (dealer) from Wollongong. I caught this bus quite often getting home from my after-school job at David Jones in Bankstown.

Preston Coburg Bus Service. Melbourne Metro. KXZ 099, a Bedford SB5 with Comair (VIC) 'square back' bodywork, built in 1973. It was one of the last two Bedfords with Comair bodies purchased by Preston-Coburg, who had exclusively operated buses bodied by them since the early 1950s.

Fairlines, Smithfield, Sydney Metro. M/O 5948, a Hino RC320 with Freighter (SA) bodywork, built in 1973. Fairlines were one of the first Sydney operators to purchase the Hino (Japan) chassis in combination with the Freighter 'Commuter' body. Freighter bodies were not common in NSW at the time and design and livery were quite attractive to me.

ACTION (ACT Interior Omnibus Network), Fyshwick, Canberra, ACT. Fleet number 218 (ZIB 218), an AEC Swift 3MP2R with Freighter (SA) bodywork, built in 1973. ACTION shortly after moved away from this coffee-coloured livery to a 'safety' yellow/orange prominent design that did reduce accidents in the network. Canberra had this body style built by three bodybuilders over various contracts.

Lewis Bros, Adelaide, SA. SUL 924, an Albion Viking (modified) with Lewis Bros (SA) bodywork, was built around 1973. Lewis Bros built their own bodies for the fleet and for other selected purchasers. They operated private services to the Adelaide suburbs, a charter business that is seen in this image, while also operating long distance services within South Australia and to the Northern Territory.

Northern Territory Bus Service, Darwin, NT. Fleet number 22 (B 802), a Hino RC 320 with Freighter (SA) bodywork, was built around 1973. These buses were built prior to air conditioning being standard on Australian buses and with Darwin tropics (the 'wet' and the 'dry' seasons) with driver glass foot vents, top and bottom sliding windows and large roof hatches.

Wallace Coaches, Hobart, Tasmania. Fleet number 11 (AR 5811), a Hino RC 320 with Motor Body Specialists (MBS, QLD) bodywork, was built around 1973. MBS made cheaper coaches than the Australian high-profile bodybuilders such as A. B. Denning, offering excellent value for money with a nice-looking body.

Langdon's Bus Lines, Myrtleford, VIC. LUX 316, a Bedford VAM 3 with Langdon's (VIC) bodywork, built in 1974. Langdon's built a few of their own bodies and this one is reasonably typical of their design. They were very plain and unattractive, in my opinion, although very practical as most in-house bodies are.

Centralian Staff Camping Tours of Australia, SA. RI 0284, a Denning Monocoque chassis with A.B. Denning (QLD) triple-deck bodywork, built in 1974. These purpose-built camping coaches were powered by an in line 6-71GM underfloor engine with large rear boot capacity for luggage and safari tents. Foodstuffs were also carried in these amazing Australian designed and built coaches.

Trans Australia Airlines (TAA), Mascot Airport, Sydney Metro. GZV 552, a Bedford VAM 3 with Freighter (SA) bodywork, built in 1974. TAA operated as one of the domestic national carriers. The Sydney-based buses were all straight deck Ford or Bedford chassis while other states were able to have a stepped deck body because they didn't have height restrictions with the city terminal. Note a Van Hool body behind.

Ventura Motors, Oakleigh, Melbourne Metro. Fleet number 26 (ICD 026), a Leyland Leopard with Freighter (SA) bodywork, built in 1974. Australian bodybuilders are boutique builders adapting to each individual operators' specification. This Freighter body has two different sized headlights that are different to the standard build options available. Ventura is one of largest Melbourne operators still trading.

Camden Coaches, Camden, Sydney Outer Metro area. MO 5687, an AEC Reliance 505 with A. B. Denning (QLD) bodywork, built in 1974. Apologies for the poor-quality image, although I felt it should be included for the British reader as it's a rare combination using the Denning 'mono' style body. I also liked the AEC chassis.

Legion Trailways, Alice Springs, NT. M/O 315 (NT), a Hino BG 100 with Freighter (SA) 'Executive' bodywork, was built around 1974. Legion was the preferred subcontractor to Ansett Pioneer for Alice Springs day tours and operated a very good tourism service. Tours to Uluru and Kata Tjuta (formerly Ayers Rock and the Olgas) were commonplace.

Public Transport Commission (PTC) Kingsgrove depot, Sydney Metro. M/O 1544, a Leyland Leopard PSU3A/2R with Mk 2 Smithfield Bus and Coach Works (Smithfield, NSW) bodywork, was built around 1975. There were slight differences between the Mk 1 and Mk 2 bodies, the Mk 2 having only one half-lantern windscreen, forced air at the top of the destination box and a few other subtle changes.

Australian Army, Randwick, Sydney Metro. 179 217, a Ford R192 with Ansair (VIC) bodywork, was built around 1974. This was the Ford that I got my army bus licence with. They were great buses that had a floor-mounted Wilson gearbox and belonged to the defunct Sydney Transport Unit at Randwick in Sydney's eastern suburbs. It is complete with 'Tac' plate and a recruiting poster.

White and Leary, Bulahdelah, NSW. M/O 208, a Bedford YRT 3 with Custom Coaches Mk 12 bodywork (Smithfield, NSW), built in 1975. The heavy-duty Bedford chassis is on a charter to the Royal Easter Show at the old Sydney showground near the Sydney Cricket Ground at Moore Park in Sydney.

Neville's Bus Service, Casula, Sydney Metro. Deregistered ex-M/O 440, a Volvo B57 with PMC Sydney bodywork, built in 1975. This all-over advertising bus displays Foster's Lager, which is quite popular in the United Kingdom but hardly anyone in Australia drinks the beer here. Foster's is more of an export market beer now and made famous by the Barry McKenzie movies.

ACTION (ACT Interior Omnibus network), Fyshwick, Canberra, ACT. Fleet number 358 (ZIB 358), a Volvo B58-56 with Smithfield Bus and Coach Works (NSW) bodywork, built in 1975. This ACT Government-designed bus had similar older bodies to the same pattern built by Freighter (SA), CVI and Smithfield when CVI left the bus building industry to concentrate on railway carriages. 358 is seen in the latter yellow safety livery.

Hornsby Coach Tours, Hornsby, Sydney Metro. M/O 405, a Bedford YRT 2 with PMC Sydney bodywork, built in 1976. This bus is what is known in NSW as a 'semi coach', the reason being that it had a jack knife door, jet air (forced air) ventilation and top sliding windows. Coaches were generally air conditioned and had a saloon (outward opening) door.

Rendell P. & G., Dubbo, NSW. MO 7341, a Bedford YRQ with Domino Hedges (QLD) bodywork, built in 1976. Domino Hedges bodies had some style about them and had their own brand logo that looked very similar to the Nissan UD bus badge. This bus operated a school run from the western regional NSW city of Dubbo to Modriguy, a village around 20 km away.

Tuck Lee Bros, Doonside, Sydney Metro. M/O 4411, a Volvo B58-56 with Superior Industries (QLD) bodywork, built in 1976. Tuck Lee operated in Sydney's western suburbs from Blacktown to a nearby suburb of Doonside. This bus is seen departing Blacktown railway station heading up to the new Kmart store that recently opened at the time. (Photo courtesy of my collection – NMP)

Batterham Coaches, Cessnock, NSW. TV 588, a Silver Eagle Series 5 with Silver Eagle bodywork, was built around 1976. Batterham's operated an express service between Cessnock (approximately 40 km inland from Newcastle) to Sydney. It was purchased from Ireland and looked magnificent when arriving at Circular Quay around 10 a.m. It is seen on a layover under the Sydney Harbour Bridge's southern pylon.

Deane's Coaches, North Ryde, Sydney Metro. M/O 5491, a Leyland National 10951/2R with Leyland bodywork assembled by PMC Sydney, built in 1976. This was the bus I drove when I had the privilege to work for the Deane family. My National was an absolute delight to drive. The heaters were so strong I could wear short sleeves during winter, although the passengers coming off cold trains and rugged up couldn't wait to get off at their stop – what fun.

Oliveri Transport, Green Valley, Sydney Metro. M/O 4193, a Leyland Leopard PSU3C/2R with PMC Sydney bodywork, built in 1977. During the 1970s the fashion for route buses were to be specified as a 'step deck', which meant more entry steps at a taller step height followed by a further step in the aisle. These were a nightmare for the off-peak passenger, who were typically mums with prams or the aged or folk with a disability.

Chapman's, Ladysmith, NSW. This deregistered Domino Tourmaster Mk 1 with Domino (QLD) bodywork built in 1977. The photo was taken after trade-in to Scania. This was a competitor to the Denning brand, having a very similar American drive train that was powered by a GM 8V71 engine. The Domino held the road better than the early Denning, although I preferred a Denning for the driver position.

Hancock Engineering, Melbourne, VIC. This new and unregistered Hancock bus chassis with Smithfield Bus and Coach Works (NSW) 'Euro' bodywork built in 1977. Hancock was an Australian designed and built chassis and around twenty were produced with Caterpillar engines and Allison automatic transmissions. They weren't popular, with the majority of chassis at the time being European manufactured.

Brisbane City Council (BCC), QLD. Fleet number 806 (806 HQA), a Volvo B59 with Domino Hedges (QLD) bodywork, built in 1977. These buses had the two-speed ZF automatic transmission as did the Panther behind the Volvo. The two BCC liveries, old and new, are visible in this photo.

Melbourne Metropolitan Tramways Board, Melbourne. Fleet number 869 (IUG 869), a Volvo B59-H50 with Ansair (VIC) bodywork, built in 1977. Have you ever seen an uglier bus? It makes an example of how the Australian Government bus evolved independently between our State and Territory bodies. Its huge destination display, which protruded a metre into the roof line, didn't make it attractive to the eye.

Ansett Pioneer (Darwin depot), NT. Fleet number 839, a Motor Coach Industries (MCI Canada) with MCI MC 8 bodywork, built in 1978. These outstanding express coaches operated around Australia, and this bus is seen on a meal stop at Three Ways at the junction of the Adelaide to Darwin (Stuart Highway) and Three Ways to Mt Isa turn off. The outback caused no issues other than the occasional stray camel, cow or kangaroo, hence the bull bar.

State Transit Authority (STA), Adelaide, SA. Fleet number 240 (STA 000), a Mercedes Benz O305 with Howard Porter (WA) bodywork, built in 1977. This bus was trialed along with a Deutz chassis with the same body to be evaluated as successors to the AEC Swift and Daimler Roadliner Adelaide fleet. Adelaide tended to be associated with MANs, although more recently with DPTI as a Scania city.

Clipper Tours, North Ryde, Sydney Metro. TV 558, a Denning Mono (monocoque) with A. B. Denning (Eagle Farm, QLD) bodywork, built in 1978. The Denning was another Australian designed and built chassis using American driveline. TV 558 was powered by a Silver 6V92T GM (303 hp) engine coupled to a six-speed Fuller box. I drove this coach regularly to the snowfields some 600 km south of Sydney.

Chester Coaches, Chester Hill, Sydney Metro. M/O 5237, a Bedford YMT 3 with Custom Coaches (Smithfield, NSW) Mk 12 bodywork, built in 1978. Chester Hill Bankstown Bus Service rebranded to Chester Coaches and launched a new 'candy stripe' livery, which was popular with coach builders at the time. This livery was a personal favourite as I grew up on this run.

Domino Industries, Brisbane, QLD. This new and unregistered Bedford BLP 2 with Domino (QLD) bodywork built in 1978. This was a show bus launched at the Sydney Bus Show and this design was extremely short-lived, with Domino having more demand for their Metroliner style on various chassis configurations. I'm ambivalent about the design.

Leyland Motors, Sydney, NSW. This new and unregistered Leyland B21 with PMC Sydney bodywork built in 1978. I'm not sure if the B21 entered the British home market. In essence, it was a Leyland National that had an inline 'pancake' underfloor GM 6-71 engine as the Leyland 501 motor proved unsuccessful in the Australian market. Repairing the Headless 501 proved unpopular with operators.

Public Transport Commission (PTC), Sydney. 37321 H (ex-M/O 1923), a Mercedes Benz O305 with PMC Sydney Mk 1 bodywork, built in 1978. This bus has been preserved by the Sydney Bus Museum members and they have done a grand job. This was the original livery for the PTC and was striking at the time. This bus was in service at the launch of the new Light Rail project from Circular Quay to Randwick in the eastern suburbs in 2019.

Ansett Pioneer (Mascot depot), Sydney Metro. Fleet number 202 (SDB 353), an RFW with Ansair (VIC) bodywork, built in 1978. RFW was another Australian designed and built chassis by Robert F. Whitehead (RFW) and had a Detroit Diesel (GM) 8V71 two stroke engine combined with a Spicer gearbox. RFW used their own Permatrak suspension and Pioneer used these coaches for Western Australian wild flower tours and Express work.

Mee's Bus Lines, Heidelberg, Melbourne Metro. ALK 977, a Bedford BLP2 with R. E. Mee bodywork (VIC), built in 1979. Mee's built for their own company and also supplied bus and coach bodies to other operators. They used lots of angles in their bodies and some like this were reasonably attractive and others were outrageous and courageous in their designs.

Punchbowl Bus Company, Riverwood. Sydney Metro. Deregistered ex-M/O 957, a Leyland Leopard PSU3E/2R with PMC Sydney bodywork, built in 1979. My daughter Eleanor is hopping off the bus in this image and having fun looking at buses. She is expecting her second baby in Jan 2020. Punchbowl have been great family friends and business associates for over thirty years.

Ansett Pioneer, Mascot, Sydney Metro. Fleet number 901 (SHR 175), a Mercedes Benz O303 with Ansair (VIC) bodywork, built in 1979. This was the first Mercedes in the fleet and Mercedes gave Ansair exclusivity for several years to build the Manheim-designed O303. The air conditioner is the bump at the front of the roof line. Wonderful chassis and ride quality.

Deanes Coaches, North Ryde, Sydney Metro. M/O 5480, an AEC Swift 760 6P2R with Domino (QLD) Metroliner bodywork, built in 1980. In Australia these AECs were known as Durban Swifts, and apparently came from a cancelled order from South Africa that was sent to Australia. These buses were head turners and so modern for their time. The 760 engine and Wilson semi-auto were fantastic to drive.

Lever Canberra Queanbeyan Charter, Queanbeyan, NSW. Fleet number 102 (MO 2), a Leyland Leopard with PMC Sydney 'Progress' bodywork, built in 1980. Queanbeyan sits on the NSW border with the ACT and Levers were known as Canberra operators of commuter buses and beautifully presented coaches. This bus is at Perisher Valley in the NSW snowfields.

Pell's Bus Service, Nambucca Heads, NSW. Fleet number 20 (MO 8879), a Bosnjak JBJ chassis with Smithfield Bus and Coach Works (NSW) 'Euro' bodywork, built in 1980. John Bosnjak of Bosnjak's Bus Service decided to build his own chassis and this bus was powered by a Mercedes engine. Engine choices included Rolls-Royce, Bedford 500 and Mercedes to name a few. He was looking for a heavy chassis with fuel efficiency. Smithfield was also owned by the Bosnjak family.

Bankstown Strathfield Bus Service, Greenacre, Sydney Metro. M/O 584, an AEC Swift 760 6PR2 with PMC Adelaide (SA) 'Commuter' bodywork, built in 1980. I owned this bus for around six years and had to sell it after having a severe stroke in 2013. This was another 'Durban Swift' and it was a magic bus to drive. My partner, selling Scania chassis, John Allen and I used to take it to the shops to buy lunch to give it a run.

Richmond Bus and Coach Service, Richmond, NSW. M/O 4578, an IBC Mk II with PMC Sydney bodywork, built in 1981. IBC (Ian and Bruce Campbell) designed and built these Australian-made chassis generally using Caterpillar engines, although this IBC had an in line 6-71GM coupled to an Allison automatic transmission. I traded this bus while at Saab Scania and sold it to an operator in Yamba on the NSW north coast.

Crawn's Motors, Burnie, TAS. BM 5219, an International C1810 with Ansair (VIC) 'Ansaliner' bodywork, built in 1982. The International C1810 had steel spring leaf suspension and had been transformed with a Volvo 10-litre engine combined with a Wilson floor-mounted semi-automatic transmission. It was a very comfortable shuttle bus when we visited Burnie on a cruise.

ACTION, Canberra. ACT. Fleet number 610, new and unregistered, is a Mercedes Benz O305 with Ansair (VIC) bodywork, built in 1982. Mercedes Benz during this period had Government fleet sales in Canberra, Sydney, Adelaide, Perth and lighter chassis being delivered into Tasmania. Mercedes sales were enormous with both Government and private operators. The O305 was particularly successful with market penetration.

Surfside, Gold Coast, QLD. 625 OHC, a Volvo B59-54 with Volgren QLD bodywork, built in 1982. Volgren used the Hess Aluminum bolted frame design and had several build plants such as Dandenong in Melbourne (Head Office), QLD, WA, New Zealand and Malaysia at their peak. Many coastal operators chose Volgren due to fewer corrosion issues.

MMTB, Melbourne, VIC. Fleet number 241 (MYD 241), a MAN SL200 with Ansair (VIC) Mk 1 body, built in 1982. Ansair, with their MMTB contracts, built ugly buses under the direction of Government engineers. The Mk 2 body introduced VoV windscreens in lieu of the earlier lantern-style screens seen here. However, beauty is in the eye of the beholder.

Moore's Tours, Kogarah, Sydney Metro. This new and unregistered rebodied Leyland Worldmaster ERT1/1 with Custom Coaches (NSW) bodywork built in 1982. This bus had a Rolls-Royce Eagle engine and the owner wanted to promote Rolls-Royce by using a stylised Rolls-Royce grill. However, Rolls-Royce weren't keen about the promotion and the grill was replaced with the standard Custom Coaches Mk 7 grill.

Westbus, Edensor Park, Sydney Metro. TV 403, a Volvo B10M with Volgren (QLD) 'Twin Deck' bodywork, built in 1984. Volgren QLD concentrated on coach production and these twin decks had a nine-seat lounge in the bottom deck, typically where a boot or rear luggage storage would be accommodated. These were known as C Series bodies and exclusive to the Volvo B10M chassis. A Chester Coaches Denning is in the background.

Makehams, Nangus, NSW. MO 1047, a Mercedes Benz OC 1617 with Ansair (VIC) bodywork, built in 1984. These coaches were used for day tours throughout the country by AAT Kings before disposal to other operators. This body was quite attractive and Makeham's were able to purchase an air-conditioned, low-km coach for a reasonable price. Nangus is in the Junee and Wagga Wagga area.

Greyhound Australia's fleet number 529 (529 PAA), a Silver Eagle Series 5 with Silver Eagle bodywork (USA), built in 1984. This coach is seen at Karuah approximately 40 km north of Newcastle at a meal stop during the fourteen-hour journey from Sydney to Brisbane. It is displaying a later livery with plenty of colour. Greyhound was the second major national express operation in Australia and the Eagles looked very modern for the time.

Punchbowl Bus and Coach Co., Riverwood, Sydney Metro. TV 340, a Leyland Tiger TRCTL11/4R with PMC Sydney bodywork, built in 1984. Arguably the ugliest coach ever built in Australia and one wonders how Leyland could have globally launched it as the world's first three-axle Tiger. I had the pleasure of driving this six-speed ZF manual during the Sydney Olympics. It's a lovely bus to drive despite its looks.

Marlin Coast Beach Bus, Cairns. QLD. This new and unregistered Hino RG197 with Austral 'Starliner' (QLD) bodywork was built around 1985. Ralph Grant was the owner of Beach Bus, who operated from Cairns to the northern beaches such as Palm Cove where many of the tourist resorts were located. He was a fabulous character and pure fun.

Brisbane City Council, QLD. Fleet number 401 (401 PQE), a Volvo B10M Mk2 with Comeng (QLD) bodywork, built in 1986. This particular bus is seen in the Cityxpress livery, which offered a limited stop service into Brisbane City. Volvo and MAN were the preferred suppliers after the Leyland and AEC era.

Fortesque Bus Service, Karratha, WA. This new and unregistered MAN 16.240 HOCL with Austral (QLD) bodywork built in 1986. Austral had an arrangement with Neoplan and one can notice the Neoplan influences, in particular the Austral name plate. The German owner was very loyal to MAN and German chassis.

Denning Stock Coach, Eagle Farm, Brisbane Metro. This new and unregistered Denning 'Landseer' with Denning (QLD) bodywork built in 1986. This was a show coach built by Denning, seen at the time as the preferred coach by Australian operators. It was Australian designed and built using American driveline and still had the two-stroke Detroit Diesel, either a V6 or V8 GM. It had a strikingly bold livery.

Sawtell Coaches, Sawtell near Coffs Harbour, NSW. TV 1168, a Scania K112TRB with Coachworks International (NZ) bodywork, built in 1986. This was the beginning of the European dominance of the coach market as the Australian-built American driveline coaches finished in liquidation or administration as sales began to fall. Mercedes had their O302, O303 and O404 range, which was the foot in the door for the other Europeans needed.

ACTION, Belconnen, Canberra Metro, ACT. Fleet number 687 (ZIB 687), a Renault PR100.2 with Ansair (VIC) bodywork, built in 1987. Renault owned Mack at the time of the French atomic testing at Moruroa Atoll and the Australian Government had diplomatic issues with France. These buses had Mack badges with the Renault Diamond to confuse the population. My fantastic wife Amanda is standing in the doorway.

Grafton Busco, Grafton, NSW. MO 0477, a MotorCoach with MCA 'Marathon' (QLD) bodywork, built in 1987. MotorCoach Australia built their own chassis and bodies using the same principles as Denning and Domino utilising American driveline, this one having a GM 6V71 engine. MCA built on other chassis, which extended their longevity before going into liquidation.

Invicta Bus Service, Croydon, Melbourne Metro, VIC. DBO 543, a Volvo B10M with Volgren (VIC) bodywork, built in 1987. The owner and staff at Invicta were hugely important to the direction taken by the Victorian market. John Usher (owner) and Geoff Peel (fleet manager) set many benchmarks. It is fair to say that Melbourne at this time was a Scania and Volvo city, the preferred chassis suppliers.

Delwood Coaches, Villawood, Sydney Metro, NSW. M/O 7647, a Roman with Custom Coaches 'Mk 85 VR' (NSW) bodywork, built in 1987. Can you believe it – a Roman in Australia. Hills Bus Sales bought two into Australia, marketing them as similar to MAN chassis. This bus proved to be so unreliable that very soon after it had a Leyland Tiger TRCTL11/3R slipped under the body.

Coachtrans, Gold Coast, QLD. This new and unregistered MAN 16.240 HOCL with GBW (QLD) bodywork was built around 1987. Coachtrans operated services between Brisbane and Coolangatta Airports with high frequency. GBW was a smaller boutique Brisbane-based bodybuilder who offered high-quality finishes from partners Leigh Gamer, Dudley Brewer and Charlie Winter. It is now known as Coach Design with another off-shoot Coach Concepts, both of which are based in and around Archerfield in Brisbane.

North and Western Bus Lines, Gladesville, Sydney Metro, NSW. M/O 972, a Leyland Tiger TRCTL11/3Rsp with PMC Sydney 'Metro 90' bodywork, built in 1988. North and Western would have had these built towards the end of the Leyland brand in Australia. The Metro 90 used VoV windscreens to enhance its look. Ken Butt, the owner, stayed with Leyland as long as he could before moving to Volvo and finally Mercedes O405 before selling to the State Transit Authority.

Murrays Coaches, Alexandria, Sydney Metro, NSW. This new and unregistered Scania K112TR with PMC Adelaide (SA) bodywork built in 1988. Saab Scania knew these as 'midi deck' coaches and the Murrays livery was so innovative for Australia at the time. These coaches were head turners with the public. Ron Murray, the owner, started this large operation from Canberra and expanded it to key tourist centres.

Howards Bus and Coach, Murrurundi, NSW. This new and unregistered (TV 897) Mercedes Benz O303/3 with Austral Tourmaster (QLD) bodywork built in 1988. Another wonderful family operation and this coach will always be known to me as the 'should have been a Scania' when I was competing for the sale. Phonse Howard had his heart set on a O303 with Tourmaster bodywork and I lost the sale.

Urban Transit Authority (UTA), Sydney, NSW. This new and unregistered (M/O 3318) Mercedes Benz O405 with PMC Sydney (NSW) Mk 5 bodywork built in 1989. Sydney at one time had the largest Mercedes fleet in the world and this bus was displayed at a Sydney Bus Show in a 1,500th delivery. The Government called them Mk 5s whereas the private companies knew them as Metro 90 bodies.

Lever Coach Lines, Queanbeyan, NSW. This new and unregistered (MO 1367) Scania K93CRB with Centurion 'Citcom' (VIC) bodywork built in 1989. This is the one and only bus that I sold to Doug and Dawn Lever sadly. I'd like to explain why but it's too embarrassing. The better story is the SAAB badge on the front, which we did locally until the Swedes arrived in Canberra and saw the bus. 'We make Scania buses, SAAB make cars. Have it removed.'

Ezi Drive Coaches, Bringelly, Sydney Metro, NSW. WEK 214, a Mercedes O302 with Jakab (Tamworth, NSW) bodywork, built in 1989. This was a rebodied chassis and in the end had a Volvo engine fitted to the bus. It was a nice smaller coach that was fitted out by Jakab. Brian and Mary Pratt were the owners of this business.

Clipper Tours, Canberra, ACT. MO 73, a Scania K113TRB with PMC Adelaide (SA) 'Apollo' bodywork, was built around 1989. This photo was taken outside Parliament House in Canberra. This Sydney-based operator expanded to Canberra and Barry Freeman drove the coach under Jim Hawkesford's direction. It was a beautiful coach to deliver and these Apollo bodies have stood the test of time with their hoop frame construction and rust proofing.

Neville's Bus Service, Casula, Sydney Metro, NSW. This new and unregistered Scania N113 with Ansair Tasmania bodywork built in 1990. These magnificent east west engine buses were state of the art and built in Tasmania. Scania and Ansair had a Tasmanian Government contract at the time based on Ansair assembling and then building on the Scania N Series chassis.

South and Western Bus Lines, Revesby, Sydney Metro, NSW. This new and unregistered (M/O 312) Leyland Worldmaster CRT2/1 with Alnor (NSW) bodywork built in 1983. Norm Stott was a partner in Alnor and worked for many years before and after with CCMC and Custom Coaches. Alnor built around five bodies before closing down. This was a rebody of an ex-STA Adelaide chassis.

Casino 99 (Richmond Bus & Coach), Richmond, NSW. This new and unregistered Scania K113TR with North Coast Bus and Coach Works (QLD) bodywork built in 1990. Because the chassis were CKD we had the flexibility to fit a K93 front overhang to permit a driver a quiet bunk area under the front stairwell. These are exciting coaches and considered innovative by myself as the Scania salesman and Allan Richardson, the owner.

Hopes Coaches, Gunnedah, NSW. This new and unregistered (MO 049) Scania K93CRB with Custom Coaches (NSW) bodywork built in 1990. This was a major change in livery for Hopes, who previously had an orange and white livery. I was a very proud salesman completing the 450 km delivery run to Gunnedah in north-west NSW.

Punchbowl Bus Co., Riverwood, Sydney Metro, NSW. M/O 4518, a MotorCoach Australia 'Citybus' chassis with MCA (QLD) bodywork, built in 1990. Joe Griffin and Steve Scott ordered this bus as it was Caterpillar powered and they could purchase aftermarket parts. The MCA arrived with much fanfare from the drivers. The chassis was in essence a prototype and hadn't been fully developed.

Punchbowl Bus Co., Riverwood, Sydney Metro, NSW. M/O 236, a Scania K93CR with PMC Sydney '160' (NSW) bodywork, built in 1990. What a marvellous family-owned company. This was my first Scania sale and we have been friends ever since – for over thirty years now. This was an order for four buses and they had the Scania automatic gearbox in them, which caused some headaches for me. The engine did over 1 million km and 'got back into warranty'.

West Bankstown Bus Service, Greenacre, Sydney Metro, NSW. This new and unregistered (M/O 5259) Cummins 844.03 with Custom Coaches (NSW) Mk 88 bodywork, built in 1991. Cummins began selling engines to the remaining American driveline bodybuilders and introduced the Csepel chassis under the Cummins brand. It wasn't successful enough to sustain the enterprise.

Sydney Buses (State Transit Authority), NSW. M/O 3411, a Scania L113TRB with Ansair (VIC) 'Orana' bodywork, built in 1993. Ansair opened a factory in Tamworth, NSW, and most of these 14.5-metre buses were delivered from Tamworth, although MO 3411 was built at Tullamarine in Melbourne. This was the first of an order for 300 Scanias including 100 CNG-powered buses. Horst Koerner is seen in the foreground.

Nicholsons, Caringbah, Sydney Metro, NSW. TV 857, a MAN 16.290 HOCL with North Coast Bus and Coach (QLD) bodywork, built in 1994. This was another of my sales when I was with MAN Automotive (AU). North Coast had to graft a Custom Coach 'Hyliner' screen into the NCBC frame. As our coaches are all custom built, North Coast accepted the challenge and built a handsome body for Neville Nicholson.

Roadcoach 'Space Liner', Sussex Inlet, NSW. This new and unregistered MAN 22.360 HOCL 14.5 metre with Austral Pacific 'Orana' (VIC) bodywork, built in 1996. This bus was purpose built for school duties and had ninety seats fitted to it. The bus was bought by Billy and Anne Smith, a lovely Scottish family who were really good to me when I was with MAN. We shared many good times and hospitality together.

Harris Park Transport, Harris Park, Sydney Metro, NSW. This deregistered Mercedes Benz O405 with Custom Coaches (NSW) Series 510 bodywork built in 1997. This bus operated a direct service to Sydney City from the north-western suburbs where no railway lines existed and was branded City Bus Direct. This was taken shortly after the owners, who have asked for privacy, sold to other companies as the NSW Government were putting too many demands on private services.

Harris Coach Tours, Parkes, NSW. This new and unregistered (TV 469) MAN 18.370 HOCL with Australian Autobus (QLD) bodywork built in 1997. This coach was owned by Paul Harris, who loved exploring unusual parts of Australia and had a huge passenger following for these tours. Australian Autobus was another bodybuilder who also built their own chassis with American driveline while also building for other OEMs. Autobus went into liquidation.

Crossley Bus Lines, Revesby, Sydney Metro, NSW. M/O 1234, a MAN 10.155 HOCL with Custom Coaches (NSW) Series 510 bodywork, built in 1997. This image is taken at Roselands, a major shopping centre in south-west Sydney, about to start the route back to Milperra via Western Sydney University. This was meant to be one of forty-one but sadly it had operational issues and remained an orphan.

Punchbowl Bus Company, Riverwood, Sydney Metro, NSW. This new and unregistered (M/O 4518) Scania L113 with Custom Coaches (NSW) CB 60 style bodywork built in 2000. These chassis were converted from CNG to diesel before being sold by myself after the CNG chassis were not ordered again by any Government agency at the time. I drove this often during the Sydney 2000 Olympics. They were great buses.

Connex NSW, Revesby depot, Sydney Metro, NSW. M/O 7984, a Scania L94UB with Bustech (QLD) bodywork, built in 2003. Connex was an early multinational company that entered the public transport sector after purchasing several private operations. Since this time the buses haven't changed much in character and uniformity is becoming the norm – and boring. The service standard improvements are questionable.

State Transit Authority, Ryde depot, Sydney Metro, NSW. Fleet number 2200 (2200 ST), a Mercedes Benz O500LE CNG with Custom Coaches (NSW) CB60 Evo 2 bodywork, built in 2010. Another example of a Government Metrobus in red livery parked at Circular Quay. The Government kept five of the contract regions, although this will soon be put to public tender and one can predict further multinationals entering the market. Passenger expectations are deteriorating – it's terribly sad now.

State Transit Authority, Waverly depot, Sydney Metro, NSW. Fleet number 2193 (2193 ST), a Volvo B12BLEA Euro 5 with Volgren (VIC) CR228L bodywork, built in 2010. This bus is on the limited stops Bondi Link 333 service to the world-famous Bondi Beach, around 7 km from Circular Quay in Sydney city. This is one of the exceptions to the supposed uniform Waratah chevron livery.

State Transit Authority, Port Botany depot, Sydney Metro, NSW. Fleet number 2766 (2766 ST), a Scania K280UB with Bustech VST (QLD) bodywork, built in 2015. The Waratah livery, as seen in the flower emblem above the letters NSW on the cant roof panel, has an added non standard moustache for 'Movember', where males are encouraged to grow moustaches for charity to help with men's health issues. Movember runs the entire month of November.

Redline (Tasmania's own), Hobart, TAS. E 24YZ (Fleet 92) Bonluck JXK6120 (China) with Bonluck body, built in 2014. These Chinese units are generally fitted with a Cummins engine and automatic gearbox. Sadly, it's the way the Australian market is heading, although Covid-19 may promote Australian manufacturing.

Ventura Motors, Dandenong depot, Melbourne Metro, VIC. Fleet number 1295 (BS 02YH), a Mercedes Benz O500LE with Volgren (VIC) 'Optimus' bodywork, built in 2017. Volgren has sold to Marco Polo from Brazil. Uniformity is spreading across the country and this is Melbourne's PTV standard livery for bus commuters in the city. All the interesting private liveries are disappearing rapidly.

Punchbowl Bus Co., Riverwood, NSW. M/O 6799 Hino Poncho HX with Hino (Japan) body, built in 2017. The NSW Government instituted an 'On Demand' service with Punchbowl on Demand (POD) operating from Bankstown Station to Bankstown Hospital. Photo taken outside my house in Padstow.

Transit Systems, Leichhardt depot, Sydney Metro, NSW. Fleet number 8106 (M/O 8106), a BYD K9RA eBus with Gemilang (Indonesia) bodywork, built in 2019. Apologies for a fuzzy speed photo, although this bus needs to be included as it is an early Chinese electric bus being trialled. The Minister of Transport has asked new contracts to offer electric bus solutions, similar to what happened in London a few years ago.

Tassielink, Hobart, TAS. XT 86 AL (Fleet 45) Scania K310B with Express Coach Builders body, built in 2019. Tassielink is a private operator servicing routes from the Tasman Peninsula, Huon Valley, and to Campania all from Hobart city. This bus is on a layover awaiting its next service.

Australia Wide Coaches, Mascot, Sydney Metro, NSW. AWC 002 'Born to Tour', a Scania K124EB with Coach Design (QLD) bodywork, built in 2000. It is photographed at the key handover with Richard Dawes, owner of Australia Wide, on the right and myself, as the Scania salesman, on the left. This day had beautiful cobalt Sydney blue skies in contrast to bush fire smoke seen in January 2020 during our devastating Australia-wide fires.

Adams Coachlines, Perth, WA. CVL 2275 (Fleet C102) Scania K124EB with Volgren (WA) 'C222TX' ody, built in 2003. This coach was in Fremantle waiting near the excellent WA Maritime Museum . It is 14.5 m long and seats fifty-six passengers in five-star comfort. It was on a day tour for Cunards's Queen Elizabeth.

State Transit Authority, Mona Vale depot, Sydney Metro, NSW. Fleet number 2852 (2852 ST), a MAN ND323F with Gemilang (Indonesia) 'Eco Double-Deck' bodywork, built in 2017. This decker has been exempted from the standard livery to promote a limited stop service from the northern beaches to Sydney city, terminating at Wynyard station. The livery is a gold colour and I believe that the variations in branding should be encouraged.

Transit Systems, Leichardt, Sydney metro. M/O 8254 (Fleet 8254) Mercedes Benz O500LE with Gemilang (Indonesia) Eco City Bus, built in 2020. This bus in seen in Eddy Ave (Sydney Central Station) after leaving Rozelle on Route 440 heading to Bondi Junction. Junctions were old tram terminus.

AAT Kings, Darwin, NT. Fleet number 132 (MO 3552), a Scania K440EB 14.5 metre with Coach Concepts (QLD) bodywork, built in 2013. This bus was doing a tour to Kakadu in the Northern Territory to see magnificent landscapes and aboriginal cultural heritage. It's an amazing tour and well worth the tourist spending some money to take it.

Mullumbus, Mullumbimby, NSW. 5876 MO Scania K270IB with Volgren 'SC222' body, built in 2008. This school bus crosses three fords on its way up to 'God's country' in the Mullumbimby range. My beautiful wife Amanda is standing next to the bus and Gary Hughes (owner) is in the bus. This was one of my babies sold to Gary.